D0553032

Grace

A Bible Study on Ephesians for Women

Keri Folmar
Cruciform Press | August 2015

To Yuri Ayliffe, Barbara Banks,
Sandhya Bharwani, Kim Blough,
Omolade Falade, Anna Harman, Kim Keliehor,
Anna Lim, Kate Nel, Catherina Ngwisha,
Naomi Njoroge, Bethany Tapp, Angela Verrips,
and Lisa Welkner.

Thank you for your wisdom, encouragement,
and prayers as we studied Ephesians together.

– Keri Folmar

CruciformPress

Praise for Keri Folmar's Inductive Bible Studies for Women

"With simple clarity, Keri Folmar guides us in learning to study the Bible…Keri encourages us to read God's Word carefully, to understand clearly, and to apply prayerfully…she encourages her readers first and foremost to listen well to God's inspired Word."

Kathleen Nielson is author of the *Living Word Bible Studies*; Director of Women's Initiatives, The Gospel Coalition; and wife of Niel, who served as President of Covenant College, 2002 to 2012.

"Keri's Bible study will not only bring the truths of [Scripture] to bear upon your life, but will also train you up for better, more effective study of any book of the Bible with her consistent use of the three questions needed in all good Bible study: Observation, Interpretation, and Application."

Connie Dever is author of *The Praise Factory* children's ministry curriculum and wife of Mark, senior pastor of Capitol Hill Baptist Church and President of 9Marks.

"It is hard to imagine a better inductive Bible study tool than this one. So many study tools wander from the biblical text, but Keri Folmar's study concentrates on what [the biblical author] says… unfolding its message with accuracy and clarity."

Diane Schreiner, the wife of SBTS professor, author, and pastor Tom Schreiner and mother of four grown children, has led women's Bible studies for more than 20 years.

"No clever stories, ancillary anecdotes, or emotional manipulation here. Keri takes us deeper into the text, deeper into the heart of [the biblical author], deeper into the mind of Christ, and deeper into our own hearts… a great study to do on your own or with others."

Kristie Anyabwile is a North Carolina native and graduate of NC State University with a degree in history. Her husband, Thabiti, serves as a pastor in Washington, DC, and as a Council Member for The Gospel Coalition.

"Keri is convinced that God is God-centered and that for the sake of our joy, we should be, too…She skillfully created these rich resources—and not only that, she has put the tools in your hands so you can study God's word for yourself…I highly recommend that you embark on these studies with some other ladies. Then you can all watch in amazement at how God gives you contentment in him."

Gloria Furman is a pastor's wife in the Middle East, and author of *Glimpses of Grace*, *Treasuring Christ When Your Hands Are Full*, and *The Pastor's Wife*.

Table of Contents

More 10-week Bible Studies for Women from Keri Folmar

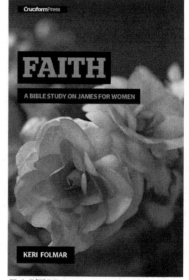

JOY!
A Bible Study on Philippians for Women

bit.ly/JoyStudy

FAITH:
A Bible Study on James for Women

bit.ly/FaithStudy

CruciformPress.com
Books of about 100 pages. Clear, inspiring, gospel-centered.

Grace - A Bible Study on Ephesians for Women

Print / PDF ISBN: 978-1-941114-07-0

As we begin this study of Ephesians, we should think through why we are studying the Bible. Why not read some other book? Or why not just get together with some other ladies and chat?

Well, have you heard the story about the kindergarten teacher who had her class paint pictures of anything they chose? One little girl was working very intently on her painting. After observing the girl for a moment, the teacher asked, "What are you painting?" The girl answered, "It's a picture of God." Amused, the teacher informed her, "No one knows what God looks like." Without looking up from her painting, the little girl responded, "They will in a minute!"

This might be a cute example of a precocious child, but many people paint pictures of God in their own minds of how God looks and acts. They "know" that God is a certain way, because they want him to be that way.

However, the one true God is transcendent. He is beyond our capacity to know. First Timothy 6:16 describes God, "[W]ho alone has immortality, who dwells in unapproachable light, whom no one has ever seen or can see." God existed before time. He is the creator, and we are his creatures. He cannot be approached by sinful man.

How can we know this God if we cannot approach him? He has to approach us. The only way to truly know God is for him to reveal himself to us. He reveals his existence and power in creation. (See Psalm 19 and Romans 1:18–21.) However, if we want to truly know this God of surpassing worth in a personal way, it must be through his Word.

And God wants us, his creatures, to know him. Jeremiah 9:23–24 says:

> Thus says the LORD: "Let not the wise man boast in his wisdom, let not the mighty man boast in his might, let not the rich man boast in his riches, but let him who boasts boast in this, that he understands and knows me, that I am the LORD who practices steadfast love, justice, and righteousness in the earth."

Do you boast in understanding and knowing the Lord? Do you want to know this God who practices love, justice, and righteousness in the earth? He wants you to understand and know him. He is ready to speak to you every morning when you wake up, throughout the day, and before you go to bed. You have only to open his Word.

A well-known catechism says, "The chief end of man is to glorify God and enjoy him forever." That is what we were created for—to truly know and enjoy the God of the universe. Jeremiah the prophet cried out: "Your words were found, and I ate them, and your words became to me a joy and the delight of my heart" (Jeremiah 15:16).

A great saint, C.H. Spurgeon, said:

> Believer! There is enough in the Bible for you to live upon forever. If you should outnumber the years of Methuselah, there would be no need for a fresh revelation; if you should live until Christ should return to the earth, there would be no necessity for the addition of a single word; if you should go down as deep as Jonah, or even descend as David said he did, into the depths of hell, still there would be enough in the Bible to comfort you without a supplementary sentence.[1]

This is why we study the Bible: it is God's revelation of himself to us. We need to know who God truly is and guard against painting our own picture of him. God has revealed himself to us not in paintings but through his Son by the words of Scripture. God the creator has spoken, and we his creation should listen to his words as life-sustaining truth and joyfully obey them.

This Bible study workbook is to assist you in studying Paul's letter to the Ephesians in an inductive way. Inductive study is reading the passage in context and asking questions of the text with the purpose of deriving the meaning and significance from the text itself. We really do this automatically every day when we read. When we study the Bible inductively we are after the author's original intent, i.e., what the author meant when he wrote the passage. In this workbook you will figure out the meaning by answering a series of questions about the text, paying close attention to the words and context of the passage.

Paul prays for the Ephesians "that the God of our Lord Jesus Christ, the Father of glory, may give you a spirit of wisdom and of revelation in the knowledge of him, having the eyes of your hearts enlightened" (Ephesians 1:17-18). Saturate your study in prayer that you would have the eyes of your hearts enlightened and your life changed as you study through this letter.

How to Do Inductive Bible Study[2]

Step 1 – **Begin with prayer.** "Open my eyes, that I may behold wondrous things out of your law" (Psalm 119:18).

Step 2 – **Read the text.**

Step 3 – Observation. *The goal of this step is to figure out what the text is saying.* This is where you ask questions like: Who? When? Where? What? These questions should be answered from the very words of the text. Ask yourself if this passage reminds you of any other passages in Scripture. Write down any questions that arise in your mind.

Step 4 – Interpretation. *The goal of this step is to figure out what the text meant to the original hearers.* This most important step is often skipped, but a lack of correct interpretation leads to incorrect application. We cannot understand what God is saying to us if we don't first understand what he was saying to his original audience and why he was saying it.

Your job in interpretation is to figure out the main point of the passage and understand the arguments that support the main point. Your interpretation should flow out of your observations, so keep asking yourself, "Can I support this interpretation based on my observations?"

Here are some questions to ask yourself as you study:

- How does the surrounding context of the passage shed light on its meaning?
- Why did the author include this particular passage in his book?

- Do other passages of Scripture fill out my interpretation?
- Is my interpretation consistent with my overall observations, or is it too dependent on a few details?
- How does this passage fit within the Bible's teaching as a whole? (The context of any passage is ultimately the Bible as a whole.)
- What is the main point of the passage?
- Can I summarize the passage in a few sentences?
- If an Old Testament passage: how does this passage relate to Christ and his work on the cross?

Step 5 – Application. *Prayerfully apply the passage to your own life.* The application should flow from the main point of the text.

Here are some questions to ask yourself in order to apply the text:

- Did I learn something new about God, his ways, his character, his plans, and his priorities? If so, how should I be living in light of this truth?
- Do I need to change my beliefs based on this passage, or is a truth reinforced?
- Is there a behavior I need to adopt or stop?
- Does this passage have implications for the way I should relate to the church?
- Does this passage have implications for the way I relate to or speak to my non-Christian friends?
- How should I pray based on this passage?
- Should I be praising God for something in this passage?
- Do I see a sin for which I need to repent?
- Is there an encouragement or promise on which I need to dwell?

In Summary

Luke 24:44–47 says,

> Then [Jesus] said to them, "These are my words that I spoke to you while I was still with you, that everything written about me in the Law of Moses and the Prophets and the Psalms must be fulfilled." Then he opened their minds to understand the Scriptures, and said to them, "Thus it is written, that the Christ should suffer and on the third day rise from the dead, and that repentance and forgiveness of sins should be proclaimed in his name to all nations, beginning from Jerusalem."

This is why we study the Bible: so that we can know Christ, repent, be forgiven, and proclaim him to the nations. We must keep Jesus in mind when we study Scripture. Adrienne Lawrence writes, "God has one overarching redemptive plan—to glorify himself by creating and redeeming a people for himself through Christ. Christ is at the center of God's plan. All of Scripture in some way speaks to that plan. Keep this in mind as you are doing your study of Scripture."

Notes

The first day of this inductive study will be an overview of Ephesians. On the following days you will study smaller segments of the letter and answer observation, interpretation, and application questions. The questions were written based on language from the English Standard Version of the Bible. However, you are welcome to use any reliable translation to do the study.

To assist you in recognizing the different types of questions asked, the questions are set out in different fonts as indicated below.

◉	**Observation:**	Look closely in order to figure out what the text is saying. Get answers directly from the text, using the words of Scripture.
✢	**Interpretation:**	What's the "true north" for this verse? Figure out what the text meant to the original hearers by determining the author's intended meaning.
♥	**Application:**	Apply the passage to your own heart and life, concentrating on the author's intended meaning that you have already determined.

Because Scripture interprets Scripture, many of the questions cite passages in addition to the one you are studying in James. If the question says, "Read…" you will need to read the additional verses cited to answer the question. If the question says, "See…" the verses help you answer the question but are not necessary. "See also…" signals you to read the verses if you would like to study the answer to the question further.

You only need your Bible to do this study of Ephesians, and in fact I highly recommend first answering the questions directly from your Bible before looking at any other materials. That said, it may be helpful for you to confirm your answers, especially if you are leading others in a group study. To check your answers or for further study, *The Message of Ephesians* by John R.W. Stott and *The Letter to the Ephesians* by Peter T. O'Brien are good commentaries.

For more general help in knowing how to study the Bible, I highly recommend *Bible Study: Following the Ways of the Word*, by

Kathleen Buswell Nielson and *Dig Deeper! Tools to Unearth the Bible's Treasure*, by Nigel Beynon and Andrew Sach. Bible study teachers and students who want a closer look at New Testament theology that will also encourage your heart can read Thomas Schreiner's, *Magnifying God in Christ: A Summary of New Testament Theology*.

Notes for Leaders

This Bible study can be done by individuals alone, but the best context for Bible study is the local church. When small groups of women gather together to study the Scriptures, it promotes unity and ignites spiritual growth within the church.

The study was designed for ladies to complete five days of "homework" and then come together to discuss their answers in a small group. The goal of gathering in small groups is to promote discussion among ladies to sharpen one another by making sure all understand the meaning of the text and can apply it to their lives. As ladies discuss, their eyes may be opened to applications of the text they didn't see while doing the individual study. Believers will encourage one another in their knowledge of the gospel, and unbelievers will hear the gospel clearly explained. As a result, ladies will learn from one another and come away from group Bible study with a deeper understanding of the text and a better knowledge of how to read the Bible on their own in their private times of study and prayer.

If you are leading a small group, you will have some extra homework to do. First, know what Bible study is and is not. Bible study is not primarily a place to meet felt needs, eat good food and chat, receive counseling, or have a free-for-all discussion. All of these things tend to happen in a ladies' Bible study, but they should not take over the focus. Bible study is digging into the Scriptures to get the true meaning of the text and applying it to lives that change as a result.

Second, make sure you know the main points of the text before leading discussion by carefully studying the passage and checking yourself using a good commentary, like one of those listed above. You may also find a Bible dictionary and concordance helpful. Second

Timothy 3:16-17 says, "All Scripture is breathed out by God and profitable for teaching, for reproof, for correction, and for training in righteousness, that the man [or woman] of God may be complete, equipped for every good work." Scripture is powerful. That power comes through truth. Scripture is not like a magical incantation where you mouth some words and see the effect. Instead, we must know what the text of Scripture means before we apply it and see its work of transformation in our lives. Your job as a discussion leader is not to directly teach, nor to simply facilitate discussion, but rather to lead ladies in finding the meaning of the text and help them see how it is "profitable" and can make them "complete, equipped for every good work."

Third, pray. Pray for the ladies in your group during the week while you prepare. Pray as you start your small group study, asking the Holy Spirit to illuminate the Scripture to your minds and apply it to your hearts. And encourage ladies to pray based on what they studied at the end of your small group time. Ask the Holy Spirit to use his sword, the Word of God, in the lives of your ladies.

Fourth, draw ladies out and keep your discussion organized. Choose what you determine are the most important questions from the study guide, focusing the bulk of your discussion on the interpretation and application questions. Ask a question, but don't answer it! Be comfortable with long pauses, or rephrase questions you think the group didn't understand. Not answering the questions yourself may be a bit awkward at first, but it will promote discussion in the end because your ladies will know they have to do the answering. Feel free to affirm good answers or sum up after ladies have had time to discuss. This gives clarity to the discussion. However, don't feel the need to fill in every detail and nuance you gleaned from your personal study. Your goal is to get your group talking.

Fifth, keep your focus on the Scriptures. The Holy Spirit uses God's Word to change ladies' hearts. Don't be afraid of wrong answers. Gently use them to clarify and teach by directing attention back to the Scriptures for the right answers. If ladies go off on unhelpful tangents, direct them back to the question and address the tangent later one on one or with reading material. However, if the tangent is on a vital question that goes to the gospel, take time to talk about it. These are God-given opportunities.

Sixth, be sure you focus on the gospel. In your prep time, ask yourself what the text has to do with the gospel and look for opportunities to ask questions to bring out the gospel. Hopefully, your church members will invite unbelievers to your study who will hear the glorious good news. But even if your group is made up of all believers, we never get beyond our need to be reminded of Christ crucified and what that means for our lives.

Lastly, enjoy studying the Scriptures with your ladies. Your love and passion for the Word of God will be contagious, and you will have the great joy of watching your ladies catch it and rejoice in the Word with you.

Paul and the Church at Ephesus

The apostle Paul identifies himself as the author of the letter to the Ephesians. Apostles were ambassadors uniquely entrusted with the message of the gospel, and Paul was specially commissioned by Jesus to take this message to the Gentiles (Acts 9:15). He traveled widely in Asia and Europe proclaiming the gospel he had once tried to destroy (Acts 8:1-3). Paul wrote the letter to the Ephesian Christians from prison.

Ephesus was a worship center for the goddess Artemis, whose pagan temple was one of the seven wonders of the world. Idolatry and magic arts were practiced there, and demon-possession was not uncommon. In the midst of this city Paul planted a church. Despite opposition and even riots over Paul's teaching, the church flourished. Ephesus became a lighthouse for the gospel in Asia Minor. Read Acts 18:18-20:1 for a full account of Paul in Ephesus and Acts 20:17-38 for Paul's exhortation to the Ephesian elders.

Begin each day this week asking God to open your eyes to the riches of his glorious grace in Christ Jesus.

When the Ephesian church received the letter from Paul, it would have been read aloud to the entire congregation. They didn't have printing presses in the first century, so a scribe would have to painstakingly copy every word. These letters were thus carefully preserved, and written copies would have been distributed to other churches to be read aloud to those congregations (See Colossians 4:16). Reading through the entire letter in one sitting is valuable to us today, not only because it gives us a feel for what happened in the first century, but also because it gives us an overview of what the letter is about as we notice certain themes repeated throughout.

Pray.

Read Ephesians 1-6.

Write down any repeated words, phrases, or ideas you notice.

What are the circumstances in Paul's life as he writes the letter?

What is the overall tone of the letter?

Write down any themes or observations that stand out to you.

Jot down any questions you have at this initial reading.

Day 2

Remember:

- 👁 **Observation:** Figure out what the text is saying. Get the answer from the words of Scripture.
- ✦ **Interpretation:** Figure out the meaning of the text. What did the writer intend to convey?
- ❤ **Application:** Prayerfully apply the passage to your own life. The application should flow from the main point of the text.

Pray.

Read Ephesians 1:1-14.

Ephesians 1:1-2

👁 1. Who wrote this letter, and how does he describe himself?

👁 2. By whose will was Paul made an apostle?

✦ 3. What does it mean that Paul was "an apostle of Christ Jesus by the will of God"? Read Acts 9:15.

👁 4. To whom was the letter written, and how are the recipients described?

✦ 5. Saint means "holy one" or "one who is set apart." It is a word the Bible commonly uses to describe those in the church. (See also Romans 1:7; Colossians 1:26; and Jude 3.) What does "in Christ Jesus" mean? Read John 17:20-26 and Galatians 2:20.

✦ 6. What was the relationship between Paul and the Ephesian Christians, and what was the atmosphere like for Christians in Ephesus? Read Acts 18:18-20:1.

♥ 7. The saints in Ephesus lived in the middle of pagan worship and persecution but had remained faithful. How have you been faithful to Christ in the midst of difficulty?

👁 8. How does Paul greet the church at Ephesus?

✦ 9. Grace means a gift that is not earned or deserved (see Romans 11:5-6). Peace occurs when two or more parties are reconciled to one another. What do you think it means for grace and peace to come "from God our Father and the Lord Jesus Christ"?

✦ 10. Why do you think Paul opens his letter with this greeting?

♥ 11. Have you received grace and peace from God the Father and the Lord Jesus Christ? If so, what difference has it made in your life? If not, go back to the verses that explain what "in Christ Jesus" means and think through what it would mean in your life to accept grace and peace from God.

Day 3

Pray.

Read Ephesians 1:3-14. (These verses were one long sentence in the Greek of the original letter.)

Ephesians 1:3-6

✦ 1. What is Paul doing in verses 3 and following?

👁 2. Who is Paul blessing and why in verse 3?

👁 3. With what has God blessed us, and in whom are we blessed?

✦ 4. Look through verses 4-14 for some of the "spiritual blessings" God has blessed us with in Christ. What are they?

✦ 5. What are some other spiritual blessings you can think of?

✦ 6. How would you explain "heavenly places" after reading verses 1:20; 2:6; 3:10; and 6:12?

♥ 7. If you are in Christ, God has blessed you with every spiritual blessing. No blessing has been withheld from you. How does that encourage you as you face difficulty or fight sin?

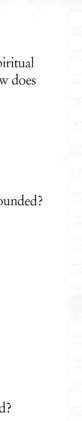

👁 8. What does verse 4 say God did before the world was founded?

✦ 9. To whom does the "us" and "we" refer?

👁 10. Why did he do this?

✦ 11. What does it mean to be holy and blameless before God?

👁 12. According to verse 5 what did God do, and for what reason did he do it?

✦ 13. What does "predestined" mean, and how does it relate to verse 4?

14. With what has God blessed us in the Beloved, and who is the Beloved?

15. What phrase in verse 6 tells us the ultimate reason for predestination?

16. What are the implications of being chosen, predestined, and adopted by God to the praise of his glorious grace? Who gets the credit for salvation? Can salvation be lost or taken away?

17. If we have been chosen to be holy and blameless sons of God, how should we live our lives?

Day 4

Pray.

Read Ephesians 1:3-14.

Ephesians 1:7-10

1. In whom and through what do we have redemption?

2. What is redemption?

👁 3. By what disposition in God do we have redemption and forgiveness?

✦ 4. Look at the word, "lavished." What does this word tell us about God's attitude toward us while we were still sinners?

👁 5. In what did God lavish the riches of his grace upon us?

👁 6. What has God made known to us?

👁 7. What is God's plan for the fullness of time, and in whom was this plan set forth?

✦ 8. What will it look like when God unites all things in him? Read Revelation 21:1-7.

✦ 9. What does redemption through Christ's blood have to do with the uniting of all things in heaven and on earth? (See also Romans 8:19-23.)

✦ 10. How do redemption and forgiveness relate to predestination?

♥ 11. We see that God through Christ accomplishes all the work of salvation. Jesus shed his blood on the cross to secure the forgiveness of sins for those God had chosen before the foundation of the world. Are you in Christ? Have you received forgiveness? If so, meditate on and rejoice in the riches of God's grace that he has lavished upon you and praise his glorious grace. If not, what questions do you have that are holding you back?

Day 5

Pray.

Read Ephesians 1:3-14.

Ephesians 1:11-14

✦ 1. To whom does the "we" in verses 11 and 12 refer? (You may want to compare it to the "you" in verse 13.)

👁 2. What have Jewish believers obtained in Christ?

✦ 3. How is this inheritance connected with the previous verses in the chapter?

✦ 4. What exactly is the inheritance? (See Psalm 16:5-6, 11; 1 Peter 2:9-10.)

👁 5. What caused the predestination of Jewish believers?

👁 6. What things does God work according to his will?

👁 7. What is the goal of having been predestined and obtaining an inheritance?

✦ 8. What do verses 11-12 tell you about God?

✦ 9. To whom does the "you" in verse 13 refer?

◉ 10. In verse 13 what two things did the Ephesian Christians do before they were sealed with the Holy Spirit?

◉ 11. What does one need to hear and believe in order to be sealed?

✦ 12. From the verses you have already studied, explain the word of truth, the gospel of salvation.

◉ 13. According to verse 14, what is it to be sealed with the Holy Spirit?

✦ 14. According to these verses, how certain is our inheritance if we hear and believe? Which words and phrases tell you of the certainty?

✦ 15. Why do you think the phrase "to the praise of his glory" is repeated twice in these verses? (See also verse 6.)

♥ 16. Have you heard and believed the word of truth? What is it that you believe?

♥ 17. Genuine believers were predestined to hope in Christ and have obtained an inheritance as God's children. How should this help you deal with trials in this life?

♥ 18. If you have believed the glorious gospel of your salvation and recognized the certainty of your inheritance, how can you live in a way that is to the praise of his glory?

Notes

Each day this week, pray for an increasing spirit of wisdom and revelation in the knowledge of Christ.

Pray.

Read Ephesians 1:3-14.

In Ephesians 1:3-14 Paul praises God for his cosmic plan and purpose of uniting all things in Christ to the praise of his glory. Paul wrote these verses as one long, exuberant sentence overflowing with praise. Let's take one more look at these verses by charting what God does, how we benefit, and God's purpose.

What has God done?	How do we benefit?	What was the purpose of God's action?
(Look for action words.) For example: v 3: Blessed us in Christ	Every spiritual blessing	(Look for linking words like *that* and *so*.) That we should be holy and blameless before him

✦ 1. Look back over your chart. What can you conclude about...

   ✦ God's Sovereignty:

   ✦ God's Purposes:

   ✦ The benefits of being adopted as sons through Jesus Christ:

♥ 2. How should this knowledge about God's sovereignty in salvation affect your evangelism?

♥ 3. How should your knowledge about God's purposes affect your priorities in life?

♥ 4. How should being adopted affect your prayer life?

Day 2

Pray.

Read Ephesians 1:3-23.

Ephesians 1:15-16

👁 1. What does Paul say he does (and does not do) in verse 16?

👁 2. What has Paul heard about the Ephesian Christians?

✦ 3. How does Paul's mention of their faith in Jesus and love for the saints connect to the verses we studied last week?

✦ 4. How are faith in Jesus and love toward the saints connected to one another?

5. Why would their faith and love cause Paul to continue to give thanks for them?

 6. Does your faith in Jesus work itself out in love for the saints in your local church? In what ways?

 7. Paul had heard about the Ephesians' love for one another. How can you love others in a way that gives you a reputation for love?

 8. Is there anyone in your church or your past whose faith and love has caused you to be thankful for her?

Pray.

Read Ephesians 1:15-23.

Ephesians 1:17-18

◉ 1. How does Paul describe God in verse 17?

◉ 2. What does he ask God to give the Ephesian Christians?

✦ 3. What does it mean to have a spirit of wisdom and revelation, and how do these things relate to one another? (See also 2 Timothy 3:14-17.)

✦ 4. How are these things found in the knowledge of God?

◉ 5. What does Paul use as a metaphor in verse 18 to describe what it is like to get this knowledge?

✦ 6. Why do you think Paul uses this metaphor? What do you think "having the eyes of your hearts enlightened" means?

👁 7. In verses 18-19 what three things does Paul pray the Ephesian Christians would know?

❤ 8. Take some time to examine your prayer life. What do you generally pray for yourself and others? What does Paul's prayer teach you about how you should pray?

Day 4

Pray.

Read Ephesians 1:15-23.

Ephesians 1:18-20

👁 1. Remind yourself: what are the three things Paul prays for the Ephesian Christians?

❤ 2. Explain the hope to which God has called the saints after re-reading verses 3-14.

♥ 3. What are some of the riches of God's glorious inheritance in the saints? See Week 1, Day 5, Question 3 for a reminder. See also Revelation 21:1-4.

♥ 4. As an analogy of suffering in the Christian life, John Newton told the story of a man who had suddenly inherited great wealth. To obtain this inheritance, which would make him more than comfortable for the rest of his life, he needs only to get to a city several miles away. On the way to the city his carriage breaks down. There is nothing for him to do except get out and walk to the city on that hot day. Will he walk to the city complaining, "My carriage is broken! My carriage is broken!"? Or will he skip to the city, rejoicing in his inheritance that will never run out with which he can buy many carriages?[3]

♥ 5. In what ways can you see yourself in this illustration?

👁 6. The third thing Paul prays for the Ephesian Christians is that they would know the "immeasurable greatness of [God's] power toward us who believe." How did God demonstrate this power in Christ (v 20)?

7. The same power that raised Christ from the dead now works in you and for you if you believe. How does this give you hope in your struggles with sin?

 8. How can this give you hope when you deal with others in their struggles with sin?

9. How could you use these verses to counsel another woman who is discouraged about her sin?

10. Why do you think Paul has prayed for the saints at Ephesus to know this power?

11. What can you do to better know "the hope to which he has called you," "the riches of his glorious inheritance in the saints," and "the immeasurable greatness of his power toward us who believe"?

Pray.

Read Ephesians 1:15-23.

Ephesians 1:20-23

👁 1. What did the working of God's great power do in Christ?

👁 2. What is Christ seated far above?

✦ 3. What does this say about the authority of Christ?

👁 4. How long will his authority last?

👁 5. What did God put under Christ's feet, and what is Christ head over?

👁 6. To whom was Christ given?

👁 7. How is the church described?

👁 8. What is the church the fullness of?

✛ 9. What does it mean for the church to be the fullness of Christ?

👁 10. Who fills all in all?

✛ 11. Write verses 22-23 in your own words.

✛ 12. What does this tell you about Christ's connection to his church?

✛ 13. What does it tell you about the importance of the church?

✛ 14. How do these verses relate to verse 10?

♥ 15. Consider your relationships in your local church. Are you committed to that body? How does your commitment of time, talents, and money show that you understand the importance of the church? What can you do to better serve your church and participate in the fullness of Christ?

Notes

Notes

This week praise God for his rich mercy and grace and pray that you would walk in the good works for which God has created you in Christ Jesus.

Pray.

Read Ephesians 1.

👁 1. The Trinity refers to the God of the Bible, who is one God in three persons: Father, Son, and Holy Spirit. Where do you see the Trinity in the following verses of chapter 1? Write down what Paul says each member of the Trinity does.

	Father	Son	Holy Spirit
3–5			
5–10			

13–14			
17			

✦ 2. How do the three persons of the Trinity work to provide every spiritual blessing?

✦ 3. What roles do each of the three persons of the Trinity perform to secure salvation for sinners?

✦ 4. What do the three persons of the Trinity have to do with adoption and inheritance?

✦ 5. How do the three persons of the Trinity act to reveal the knowledge of God?

♥ 6. How does (or should) this doctrine of the Trinity affect how you see the Christian religion? Is it about following rules or a relationship with the living God?

♥ 7. How does knowing that God the Father has been a Father from eternity past—Fatherhood is part of his character—affect your prayer life?

 8. How does the Trinity affect the way you seek to know God? (See John 14:8-11.)

♥ 9. How does the Trinity affect your hope for the future?

The triune God does what no other could: the Father sends us what is most precious to him, his Son; and the Son, uniting us to himself by the Spirit, brings us back before his Father to share the relationship he has always enjoyed. This God shares himself; we are brought into the very life of this God; we are given the Son's own Comforter to be our own, and given the Son's own right to cry "Abba" (Galatians 4:4-6). More than forgiveness, more than paradise, Christians share the Son's own indestructible standing and intimacy before the Father. No other god could give us so much.… In the triune God we find the only God who is love, we find a God who welcomes in the failures, sharing with them all he has to offer: his own eternal life, love, joy and comfort.[4]

Day 2

Pray.

Read Ephesians 2.

Ephesians 2:1-3

✦ 1. To whom does the "you" in verse 1 refer?

👁 2. In what did you once walk?

👁 3. In what state of existence were you in those trespasses and sins?

👁 4. What and whom were you following?

✦ 5. Who is this spirit that is at work in the sons of disobedience?

👁 6. In what way did we all once live?

✦ 7. How do "the course of this world" and "the prince of the power of the air" relate to "the passions of our flesh"?

👁 8. Who were we by nature?

✦ 9. What does it mean to be "children of wrath"? (Whose wrath is it?)

✦ 10. What is the state of every person who is not made alive with Christ?

✦ 11. Write verses 1-3 in your own words.

✦ 12. Can a person who has no spiritual pulse become spiritual on her own? Why or why not?

♥ 13. We end this day's study with very bad news. The dead person can do nothing to help herself. Unbelievers are like zombies following the philosophies of the world, obeying the devil and being driven by their selfish desires. They are without hope in this world. If you believe this bad news, what should your priorities be with friends and family who are dead in their trespasses and sins?

♥ 14. If the bad news is true, what should your priorities be toward people in parts of the world who have never heard the good news? How can you participate in getting the good news out to them?

Pray.

Read Ephesians 2:1-10.

Ephesians 2:4-7

◉ 1. Yesterday we read the bad news that as unbelievers we are dead in our trespasses and sins. What are the first two words of verse 4?

✦ 2. Who is acting in response to spiritual deadness?

◉ 3. In what is God rich, and why is he acting?

◉ 4. When did God love us?

✦ 5. What was lovable about us then? Read Romans 5:8.

♥ 6. Do you remember being dead, living in the passions of your flesh? What stands out for you about your former life?

👁 7. What has God done out of his love?

✦ 8. What does it mean to be made "alive together with Christ"? (See also Galatians 2:20 and 1 Peter 1:3-5.)

♥ 9. In what ways can you testify to being made alive with Christ?

👁 10. If you are a Christian, by what have you been saved?

👁 11. When God "made us alive together with Christ," what else did he do?

✦ 12. What does it mean for us that God raised us up and seated us with Christ in the heavenly places?

♥ 13. Remembering your former life (vv 1-3) and your current blessings (vv 4-7), how does your heart respond?

👁 14. Why did God make us alive, raise us up, and seat us with him in Christ?

✦ 15. How does the fact that God raised us up with Christ show the immeasurable riches of his grace in kindness?

✦ 16. In the previous chapter, the praise of God's glory is given as the purpose for our adoption and our inheritance (vv 6, 12, and 14). What does showing the ultimate riches of God's grace have to do with his glory? Why is it important for God to show the riches of his grace in Christ Jesus?

♥ 17. When God shows you the immeasurable riches of his grace, how does it benefit you? Do you marvel at God's grace in his kindness toward you? Does this bring you joy?

♥ 18. How can your life more fully showcase the immeasurable riches of God's grace?

Day 4

Pray.

Read Ephesians 2:1-10.

Ephesians 2:8-9

👁 1. By what have you been saved?

✦ 2. What does "grace" mean?

👁 3. Through what are you saved?

✦ 4. According to previous verses in Ephesians, from what are you saved?

✦ 5. What does "faith" mean, and what is the object of faith? In other words, what must we have faith in? (Read Ephesians 1:13.)

👁 6. Where do we get the grace that saves through faith? Where does it not come from?

👁 7. Why can no one boast about her own salvation? (Look at the clauses both before and after the phrase about boasting.)

🖤 8. If we believe in Christ and know that grace and faith come as gifts from God, how should we regard ourselves?

🖤 9. If grace and faith come as gifts from God, how should we treat those who do not believe?

🖤 10. How should these truths affect our evangelism?

Day 5

Pray.

Read Ephesians 2:1-10.

Ephesians 2:10

👁 1. What are we, and in whom were we created?

✦ 2. What does it mean to be created in Christ Jesus? Do any previous verses we've studied help with this question?

👁 3. For what purpose were we created?

👁 4. What is God's part in good works, and what is our part?

✦ 5. Write verse 10 in your own words.

 6. How do verses 8-10 give you purpose in life?

7. What are the implications for your life if God has already prepared good works for you to do?

8. How can you walk in the good works God has prepared for you?

9. You were dead in your sins, but God in his grace has made you alive in Christ to showcase his kindness. God has also prepared good works for you to do. Give God thanks for his mercy, grace, kindness, and love, praying for a heart that delights to walk in the good works he has prepared for you.

Notes

Notes

This week pray each day for your church to be "built on the foundation of the apostles and prophets, Christ Jesus himself being the cornerstone" (v 20).

Pray.

Read Ephesians 2.

Ephesians 2:11-13

✦ 1. What does "therefore" refer back to? (What is the "therefore" there for?)

◉ 2. What are Gentiles called by those who are called "the circumcision"?

◉ 3. How is circumcision made? (Note: Circumcision is cutting off the foreskin of the male reproductive organ. This was done in Israel to every male child eight days after birth to mark them as part of the covenant community of God's people.)

✦ 4. Why does Paul emphasize that the Ephesians are Gentiles "in the flesh" and that circumcision is made "in the flesh by hands"?

👁 5. What does Paul tell the Ephesian Christians to remember?

✦ 6. What does it mean for the Ephesian Christians to have been "alienated from the commonwealth of Israel and strangers to the covenants of promise"? Read Genesis 17:4-8 and Exodus 19:5-6.

👁 7. What hope does one have who is separated from Christ?

✦ 8. How are verses 11-12 related to verses 1-3?

👁 9. "But now" what has happened for those who are in Christ?

✦ 10. To whom are those in Christ brought near?

👁 11. By what are those in Christ brought near?

✦ 12. What does "the blood of Christ" refer to? (See also Hebrews 9:22-26.)

♥ 13. Refer back to the exhortation given to Israel in Exodus 19:5-6 and read 1 Peter 2:9-10. Peter uses the passage in Exodus to describe the church. Because of the blood of Christ, Gentile believers are now part of God's people. Do you think of your local church as God's treasured possession? In what ways do you treat your church as his treasured possession?

♥ 14. In what ways can you grow in this area?

Day 2

Pray.

Read Ephesians 2.

Ephesians 2:14-16

👁 1. Who is our peace?

◉ 2. What has Christ made us, and what has he broken down?

◉ 3. In what (or by what) did he break down the wall of hostility, and what did he abolish?

✦ 4. In Matthew 5:17 Jesus said, "I have not come to abolish [the Law or the Prophets] but to fulfill them." Read Matthew 5:17-20 and Colossians 2:13-23. In light of these verses, how do you reconcile Matthew 5:17 and Ephesians 2:15?

◉ 5. Why did Christ break down the dividing wall and abolish the law of commandments and ordinances?

✦ 6. Verses 14-16 refer to "both" and "two." What are the two groups of people Paul is talking about? (See verse 11.)

◉ 7. To whom were both Jews and Gentiles reconciled, and through what were they reconciled?

✦ 8. Based on verse 16, how are both Jews and Gentiles saved and brought to God the Father? (See also John 14:6-7.)

👁 9. Jesus was killed on the cross. What else was killed there?

💜 10. Jesus' death on the cross made peace, so much so that people who were once hostile to one another are now called "one new man" and "one body." What does this tell you about the importance of unity among diversity in a local church?

💜 11. What does this suggest about ethnic or socio-economic distinctions in a local church?

💜 12. What are some things that bring disunity in a local church?

💜 13. What are some things you can do to promote unity in your church?

Pray.

Read Ephesians 2:11-22.

Ephesians 2:17-20a

👁 1. What and to whom did Jesus preach?

✦ 2. Who are those "far off, and who are "near"?

👁 3. To whom do both Jews and Gentiles have access through Jesus? And in whom do we have this access?

✦ 4. How did Jesus make a way for us to have access to the Father?

✦ 5. What does it mean for us to have access to the Father?

👁 6. What are the Ephesian believers no longer? And what have they become?

✦ 7. What do each of these words suggest: Citizens? Saints? Members of the household of God?

👁 8. Upon what is this household built?

✦ 9. What does it mean for the church to be "built on the foundation of the apostles and prophets"? (Read Acts 1:21-26; 2:42-43; 10:43; and Revelation 21:14.)

♥ 10. What does this suggest about how unity is built and kept in the church?

♥ 11. What does this suggest about the central focus of the local gathering of the church?

♥ 12. What does this suggest about the importance of Scripture in your own life?

Pray.

Read Ephesians 2:11-22.

Ephesians 2:20-22

👁 1. Who is the cornerstone of the church?

✦ 2. What is a cornerstone? What does it mean for Christ Jesus himself to be the cornerstone?

👁 3. How does verse 21 further describe what it means for Jesus to be the cornerstone?

✦ 4. The temple was the place where God dwelt with his people in the Old Testament. What does it mean for the household of God to be "a holy temple in the Lord"?

✦ 5. God is omnipresent—He is everywhere. How is his dwelling with the church different than the way he is present everywhere else?

👁 6. In Christ, what is happening to the saints at Ephesus?

✤ 7. Who is doing the building?

✤ 8. How does the Holy Spirit work to make a church a dwelling place for God? (See John 4:21-24 and 2 Corinthians 6:16-7:1.)

♥ 9. If your church is the household of God and a dwelling place for God, what should your attitude toward it be? What should your commitment level be?

♥ 10. What does Christ Jesus being the cornerstone suggest about how unity is built in a local church?

♥ 11. How can a church keep Christ as the central focus?

♥ 12. How can you keep Jesus central in your life?

Day 5

Pray.

Read Ephesians 2:11-3:6.

Ephesians 3:1-6

👁 1. Where is Paul?

👁 2. Why is he there?

✦ 3. Paul writes, "For this reason," but then breaks his train of thought to resume it in verse 14 where he repeats, "For this reason." We'll come back to this in verse 14, but for now, what does "this reason" refer back to in the previous verses?

👁 4. What does Paul assume the Ephesian Christians have heard?

✦ 5. Paul has written briefly in chapter 1:9-10 of the mystery made known to him by revelation. What is this stewardship of God's grace given to Paul for the Gentiles?

✦ 6. A mystery is something that was not known but now has been revealed. What does Paul mean when he says that the mystery of Christ was not known to previous generations but now has been revealed to apostles and prophets?

👁 7. What is the mystery according to verse 6?

✦ 8. Why do you think the unity of Jews and Gentiles in the church has been repeatedly emphasized in chapters 1, 2, and 3?

♥ 9. Have you seen disunity in your church between different ethnic groups? What about different socio-economic groups? What about age or stage of life groups?

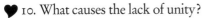

♥ 10. What causes the lack of unity?

♥ 11. How can you personally work for unity in your church?

♥ 12. Some churches may have a great deal of unity because everyone is from the same ethnic and socio-economic background. Maybe everyone is also the same age or in the same stage of life. Some churches even have separate services for these different groups. Based on what you have read in Ephesians so far, why do you think it is important for churches like this to reach out and bring in people who add diversity? (See also Revelation 7:9-10.)

Notes

This week pray to comprehend the breadth, length, height, and depth of the love of Christ, and pray for the manifold wisdom of God to be made known through the church.

Pray.

Read Ephesians 3.

Ephesians 3:7-9

◉ 1. Of what and according to what was Paul made a minister?

◉ 2. How was God's grace given to Paul?

✦ 3. To what working of God's power is Paul referring? Read Acts 9:1-19.

◉ 4. How does Paul describe himself?

✦ 5. Why does Paul describe himself this way? Read 1 Corinthians 15:9.

👁 6. What is the grace that was given to Paul?

✛ 7. Paul went through many trials and persecutions to preach the gospel to the Gentiles. (You can read about some of them in 2 Corinthians 11:23-33.) Why would he still describe preaching the gospel as a gift from God?

✛ 8. Paul speaks of the riches of Christ as immeasurable (2:7) and unsearchable (3:8). Why would his valuation of knowing Christ overflow into sharing Christ?

♥ 9. Discuss whether you think of sharing the gospel as a gift from God.

♥ 10. What fears hold you back from sharing the gospel?

♥ 11. What motivates you to share the gospel?

✦ 12. Take a moment to write out a brief summary of the gospel message, perhaps using some verses from Ephesians.

♥ 13. What motivates you to share the gospel?

Day 2

Pray.

Read Ephesians 3.

Ephesians 3:10

👁 1. For what purpose was Paul given the gift of preaching to the Gentiles?

✦ 2. Who are the rulers and authorities in the heavenly places? Read Ephesians 6:12 and 1 Peter 1:12.)

✦ 3. Manifold means multifaceted and varied. Dwell on the phrase "manifold wisdom of God" for a moment. The manifold wisdom of God is made known in the heavenly places through the church!

✦ 4. How is God's manifold wisdom shown by diversity in the church? (Think about ethnic, socio-economic, age, and stage of life.)

✦ 5. How is God's manifold wisdom shown in the individual testimonies and life circumstances of those who gather in the church?

✦ 6. How is God's manifold wisdom shown in different personalities, abilities, and giftings in the church?

♥ 7. Can you think of ways God's manifold wisdom is shown in your local church?

8. How does local church membership, as opposed to haphazard or low-commitment attendance, sharpen the display of God's wisdom?

9. Does it cause you to rejoice that your local church would display God's manifold wisdom to rulers and authorities in the heavenly places? How can you be more a part of this display?

Day 3

Pray.

Read Ephesians 3.

Ephesians 3:11-13

1. What does "This" in verse 11 refer to?

2. In whom was God's eternal purpose realized?

✦ 3. What is God's eternal purpose (v 11), and how does this verse relate to Ephesians 1:7-10?

✦ 4. What does it mean that God's eternal purpose was "realized" in Christ Jesus?

✦ 5. What can you conclude about God's plan from verse 11?

👁 6. What do we have in Christ Jesus our Lord?

✦ 7. To whom do we have access?

👁 8. How do we gain the access to God in Christ Jesus?

✦ 9. What does it mean to "have boldness and access with confidence" to God?

♥ 10. Why would the gospel being God's *eternal* purpose *realized* in Christ Jesus increase our boldness and confidence toward God?

♥ 11. How should verses 11-12 affect your prayer life?

♥ 12. How should verses 11-12 affect the way you approach God when you sin?

👁 13. What does Paul not want the Ephesian Christians to lose heart over?

✦ 14. What is Paul suffering?

✦ 15. Why would Paul's suffering be their glory?

♥ 16. Do you desire the glory of God and the glory of others above your own comfort? What does this verse say to you about sharing the gospel when the circumstances aren't easy?

Day 4

Pray.

Read Ephesians 3.

Ephesians 3:14-17

✦ 1. In verse 1 of chapter 3, Paul wrote, "For this reason," but then he broke his chain of thought to write verses 2-13. Now in verse 14 he comes back and uses the phrase again. What does "this reason" refer to in the verses before chapter 3 (see Week 4, Day 5, Question 3), and how did verses 2-13 further illuminate the reason?

👁 2. What does "this reason" cause Paul to do?

👁 3. How does Paul describe the Father?

✦ 4. Why do you think he uses this description?

👁 5. In Paul's prayer, we basically read two main petitions for
strength that culminate in an ultimate goal for the Ephesian
Christians. What are the two main petitions and what is the
ultimate goal?

👁 6. Regarding the first petition, from what reserves will God grant
the Ephesian Christians strength?

✦ 7. We've seen language similar to this in previous verses like 1:7;
1:18; 2:7; and 3:8. What does this language tell you about God's
ability to grant this power?

👁 8. Through whom does this strengthening come, and where is the
strengthening?

✦ 9. Verse 17 adds a parallel phrase describing how God strengthens
the believer. What are the parallels between the phrases, "power
through his Spirit in your inner being" and "so that Christ may
dwell in your hearts"?

👁 10. What is the vehicle through which Christ dwells in the hearts
of believers?

✦ 11. Christ already dwells in the heart of every believer by the Holy Spirit (1:13-14). Why do you think Paul prays this prayer? (From where does strength for the believer come?)

👁 12. What will result from this strengthening of Christ dwelling in their hearts?

✦ 13. What does it mean to be rooted and grounded in love?

✦ 14. Considering what you have read previously in Ephesians (Paul is praying "For this reason"), why do the Ephesian Christians need this strengthening and grounding in love?

♥ 15. What do you need strength for right now?

♥ 16. God can grant you strength that results in you being rooted and grounded in love out of the vast riches of his glory, as Christ dwells in your heart through faith. Pray for the strength you need in the particular circumstances you mentioned above.

Day 5

Pray.

Read Ephesians 3:11-21.

Ephesians 3:18-19

👁 1. Regarding Paul's second petition, in what ways does he want the Ephesian Christians to comprehend God's love?

✦ 2. What is Paul doing when he gives these geometrical parameters to the love of God?

👁 3. What surpasses knowledge?

✦ 4. How can Paul pray for the Ephesian Christians and all the saints to know the love of Christ if it surpasses knowledge? What is he trying to say when he writes these words?

✦ 5. How does being rooted and grounded in love form the foundation of knowing the love of Christ?

♥ 6. How do Christians increase their knowledge and understanding of the love of Christ? What can you do to increase yours?

♥ 7. Write what you know of the love of Christ. How would you describe it to a friend?

 8. What is the ultimate result for which Paul prays?

✦ 9. What does it mean to be filled with the fullness of God?

✦ 10. How do being strengthened by the indwelling of Christ and knowing the love of Christ lead to being filled with all the fullness of God?

✦ 11. Go back and read Paul's previous prayer in 1:16-23. How does that prayer and this one in 3:16-19 relate to one another?

✦ 12. After examining these prayers, what would you say is Paul's goal for Christians?

♥ 13. What should be your goal for yourself and other saints in your church? What means should you use to work toward this goal?

♥ 14. Do you pray like Paul? How should these prayers of Paul inform the way you pray for yourself and others?

Notes

This week pray that you would "walk in a manner worthy of the calling to which you have been called" (4:1) and that your church would "grow up in every way into him who is the head, into Christ" (4:15).

Pray.

Read Ephesians 3:14-4:16.

Ephesians 3:20-4:1

♥ 1. After studying Paul's prayer last week, did you feel excited about what God is doing in you and in your church, or did you get discouraged because you don't feel strong and rooted and filled?

👁 2. We have much reason for hope that ultimately we will be filled with the fullness of God. What does verse 20 tell us God is able to do, and according to what power does he do it?

✦ 3. What is that power? (Remember 1:19-20 and 3:16-17.)

♥ 4. Have you ever prayed for your spiritual good or someone else's and God has done abundantly more than you asked or thought? Describe the situation.

👁 5. What does verse 21 tell us is the ultimate goal?

♥ 6. Does this ultimate goal give you even more confidence that God will do abundantly more than you ask or think? Why or why not?

✛ 7. What do these verses imply about whether we need to know God's specific will in particular circumstances in order to pray accurately?

♥ 8. How does verse 20 cause you to give God glory in the church and in Christ Jesus?

✦ 9. In chapters 1-3, Paul has taught glorious truths about the gospel and what it means to be in Christ. He has also prayed for the Ephesian church. This is typical of Paul's letters: He prays and teaches doctrine, then he exhorts the church to live in a manner worthy of the gospel. Why do you think this order is so important?

♥ 10. What does this tell you about how children should be taught about Christian living?

♥ 11. What does it tell you about how to motivate yourself or others toward greater obedience?

Day 2

Pray.

Read Ephesians 3:20-4:16.

Ephesians 4:1-3

✦ 1. What does "therefore" refer to in verse 1? (What is the "therefore" there for?)

◉ 2. What does Paul urge the Ephesian Christians to do?

✦ 3. Why do you think Paul reminds the Ephesian Christians that he is a prisoner for the Lord at this point in his letter?

✦ 4. What is the calling to which the Ephesian Christians have been called? (See Ephesians 1:3-6.)

✦ 5. What does Paul mean when he uses the term "walk"?

◉ 6. How is this manner further described in verses 2-3?

✦ 7. What are humility and gentleness?

✦ 8. What does it mean to be patient and bear with one another in love?

✦ 9. How do these qualities help one to maintain unity and peace?

✦ 10. What relationships is Paul concerned with here? In other words, between whom does he want to ensure the unity and peace? Point to specific words in the verses for evidence.

♥ 11. Are you eager to maintain unity and peace in your church?

♥ 12. In what ways can you show more humility and gentleness? (Are there areas or situations in your church where you are irritable or insist on your own way?)

♥ 13. Is there a particular situation or person with whom you need patience? How can you exercise humility and gentleness or bear with the person in love?

Day 3

Pray.

Read Ephesians 4:1-16.

Ephesians 4:4-12

👁 1. List the things Paul says there is one of.

✦ 2. Why do you think Paul lists these "ones"? What point is he trying to make?

👁 3. How is the one God and Father described?

✦ 4. What does it mean that God "is over all and through all and in all"?

✦ 5. What does the list of ones and the description of God the Father have to do with walking in a worthy manner?

👁 6. To whom was grace given, and according to what was it given?

✦ 7. After focusing on the unity of "all," Paul now turns to "each one." What kind of grace is Paul writing about in verse 7?

✦ 8. In verse 8, Paul quotes Psalm 68:18. The Psalm celebrates God's care for Israel in driving away their enemies and instituting his rule on Mt. Zion. Verse 18 describes God ascending to victory and receiving the spoils of those he has defeated. Paul applies this verse to Jesus, having ascended into heaven, distributing the spoils of victory to his people. After reading Psalm 68, describe what "Christ's gift" is and what it would mean for him to give gifts to the church.

👁 9. Christ descending into "the lower regions, the earth," refers to the Son of God taking on human flesh, becoming man and ultimately dying. Christ "ascending" refers to his resurrection and ascension into heaven (Acts 2:32-33; Hebrews 7:26). According to verse 10, what is the result of his descending and ascending?

✦ 10. What does it mean for Christ to fill all things? How does this verse relate to 1:22-23 and 3:19?

👁 11. According to verse 11, what has Christ given?

✦ 12. What do these gifts have in common?

👁 13. Why did Christ give these gifts?

👁 14. What is the work of ministry for?

✦ 15. The gifts mentioned in verse 11 all relate to proclaiming God's Word. Tomorrow we will examine further the importance of these gifts. Many other spiritual gifts are mentioned in Scripture, but there is one purpose for all gifts. What is the purpose mentioned here and in 1 Corinthians 12:4-7?

♥ 16. In many cultures, we tend to see spiritual gifts as entitlements. "God has gifted me, and I am entitled to exercise my gift in my church." How do these verses work against an individualistic attitude of entitlement? What should our attitude be about exercising our gifts?

♥ 17. Verse 7 says, "Grace was given to each one of us." How are you using your gifts for building up the body of Christ? Is there a need in your church that you can meet?

Day 4

Pray.

Read Ephesians 4:1-16.

Ephesians 4:11-14

✝ 1. Remind yourself: what do the gifts mentioned in verse 11 have in common?

👁 2. What do these gifts do?

👁 3. What is the work of ministry for?

👁 4. What is the ultimate goal of teaching in the church?

✦ 5. What would it mean to be unified in faith and knowledge of the Son of God?

👁 6. What (or who) is the measure of mature manhood?

✦ 7. How do faith and knowledge cause maturity?

👁 8. What does Paul want to make sure the church is not?

👁 9. What happens to children?

✦ 10. According to these verses, why is Word-centered teaching so important to the church?

✦ 11. What is the unity Paul writes about centered on?

♥ 12. How much importance do you place on being taught rightly from the Word? Do you prioritize sitting under the preaching of God's Word? Do you take advantage of Bible, theology, or Christian living classes at your church?

♥ 13. If you teach other women or children at your church, how hard do you strive to teach right doctrine? Do you set aside plenty of time for preparation and made sure you are a student of the Scriptures yourself?

♥ 14. What is most important to you in a church? (Do you look first for right doctrine and Word-centered teaching, or do you have other priorities?)

Pray.

Read Ephesians 4:1-16.

Ephesians 4:15-16

👁 1. What does Paul contrast with being children tossed to and fro?

👁 2. How does a church grow up?

✦ 3. Some people use the phrase, "speaking the truth in love," when they want to rebuke someone else or say something harsh. Looking at the phrase in the context of verse 11-16, what does it mean?

✦ 4. How are sound teaching and love related? (See also Philippians 1:9-11.)

✦ 5. What does it mean for Christ to be the head of the church?

👁 6. What does the church need to work properly?

👁 7. What is the church built up in?

✦ 8. Paul's body analogy illustrates the priority of Christ as the head. How does it illustrate the importance of each individual member of the church?

✦ 9. How does teaching ensure that each part of the church body is working properly?

♥ 10. How are the priorities of truth and love played out in your church?

♥ 11. Are you praying for those who teach the Word in your church? Knowing the vital importance of these gifts for equipping the saints, how can you better support those who teach?

♥ 12. How are you participating in building up your church? How can you better participate?

Notes

Pray this week to put off the old self and put on the new self.

Pray.

Read Ephesians 4.

Ephesians 4:17-19

✦ 1. Why does Paul begin this section with "Now"? What has he done in the previous chapters and verses and what is he about to do?

◉ 2. What is Paul's command to the Ephesian Christians?

◉ 3. How do the Gentiles walk?

◉ 4. What are they darkened in, and what are they alienated from?

◉ 5. Why are they alienated from the life of God?

◉ 6. What has caused their ignorance?

✦ 7. What does it mean for the Gentiles' minds to be futile?

✦ 8. How would hardness of heart keep someone in a state of ignorance?

✦ 9. How would ignorance alienate someone from the life of God?

👁 10. What have the Gentiles become, and what have they given themselves up to?

✦ 11. How does this description of the Gentiles correspond to 2:3?

✦ 12. Why is Paul describing how the Gentiles live? What does that have to do with the Ephesian Christians?

♥ 13. How is looking outside the church at how the world lives instructive to us as Christians?

♥ 14. Knowing that we once were darkened in our understanding, alienated from the life of God, what should our attitude be toward unbelievers?

♥ 15. What should our attitude be toward the culture in which we live? Discuss whether we should expect perfect righteousness and justice in this world or work toward righteousness and justice, knowing that our hope is not in any culture or government but is in heaven?

Day 2

Pray.

Read Ephesians 4:17-32.

Ephesians 4:20-24

👁 1. What does Paul contrast with the way the unbelieving world walks?

👁 2. What does Paul assume?

👁 3. Who is the truth in?

✦ 4. What is this truth contrasted with in verses 17-18?

👁 5. What do verses 22-24 say the Ephesian Christians were taught to do in Jesus?

👁 6. How is the "old self" described?

✦ 7. How does this description correspond to the description of the Gentiles and 2:3?

✦ 8. What does it mean to put off the old self?

✦ 9. What does it mean "to be renewed in the spirit of your minds," and how does this contrast with the futility of the minds of the Gentiles that are darkened and ignorant? (See also Romans 8:28 and 12:2.)

👁 10. How is the new self described?

✦ 11. What does it mean for the new self to be "created after the likeness of God"?

✦ 12. How does this description relate to 2:10?

♥ 13. How can you work to put off the old self?

♥ 14. How can you "be renewed in the spirit of your mind"?

♥ 15. How can you work to put on the new self?

✦ 16. The new self of the believer has already been created. We are God's "workmanship, created in Christ Jesus for good works, which God prepared beforehand, that we should walk in them" (2:10). Discuss how these verses assume both personal responsibility and God's sovereignty.

♥ 17. How do these verses spur you on to "walk in a manner worthy of the calling to which you have been called" (4:1)?

Day 3

Pray.

Read Ephesians 4:17-32.

Ephesians 4:25-28

✦ 1. What is the "Therefore" there for?

👁 2. What have the Ephesian Christians put away, and what are they to speak?

👁 3. Why are they to speak the truth to their neighbors?

✦ 4. How is Paul using the word, "neighbor"? Based on the description of a neighbor, to whom is he referring?

✦ 5. What does it mean that the Ephesian Christians have put away falsehood? How does this relate to verses 17-24?

✦ 6. What does it mean to speak the truth? (Does it just mean to not lie?)

✦ 7. What does this command have to do with being "members of one another"?

👁 8. What does Paul command in verse 26?

✦ 9. How can one be angry and not sin?

✦ 10. What makes some (if not most) anger sinful?

👁 11. Why should the Ephesian Christians not let the sun go down on their anger?

✦ 12. When Paul says, "do not let the sun go down on your anger," what principle is he trying to get across, and what does the devil have to do with it?

👁 13. What does Paul command in verse 28?

👁 14. Why should the thief labor instead of stealing?

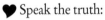 15. How do the three commands in verses 25-28 help keep unity in the church?

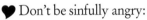 Speak the truth:

 Don't be sinfully angry:

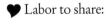 Labor to share:

♥ 16. How are you doing in each of these areas?

♥ Speak the truth:

♥ Don't be sinfully angry:

♥ Labor to share:

Pray.

Read Ephesians 4:17-32.

Ephesians 4:29-30

👁 1. What does Paul prohibit in verse 29?

👁 2. What kind of talk does Paul commend?

👁 3. Why does he commend this kind of talk?

✦ 4. What kind of talk would be corrupt?

✦ 5. What does it mean for talk to "fit the occasion"?

✦ 6. What kind of talk builds others up in the church, giving them grace?

✦ 7. Why is our speech so important? Read Matthew 12:33-37 and James 3:8-12.

✦ 8. Why does Paul bring up speech here in his letter? What does speech have to do with unity in the church?

👁 9. What does Paul write not to do in verse 30?

👁 10. How does he describe the Holy Spirit?

✦ 11. Looking at the overall context of these verses and the detailed commands, how might a Christian grieve the Holy Spirit?

✦ 12. What does the fact that the Holy Spirit can feel sadness over the actions of a believer tell you about him?

✦13. What does it tell you about the importance of unity in the church?

♥ 14. What type of corrupt talk do you struggle with?

♥ 15. What kind of talk do you use to build others up at your church?

♥ 16. Considering Matthew 12:33-37, what are some ways you can work on both putting off corrupt talk and putting on gracious talk?

Day 5

Pray.

Read Ephesians 4:17-32.

Ephesians 4:31-5:2

1. What does Paul write to put away from you?

2. How much of it are we to put away?

3. Define each of these characteristics.

Bitterness:

Wrath:

Anger:

Clamor:

Slander:

✦ Malice:

♥ 4. Now search your heart. With which of these do you most struggle?

♥ 5. Are any of these sins affecting your relationships in the church?

👁 6. How does Paul say we should treat one another?

✦ 7. What does it mean to be kind and tenderhearted toward one another?

✦ 8. Why might we need to forgive one another in a church?

👁 9. How are we to forgive one another?

✦ 10. How is God's forgiveness the basis on which we forgive others?

✦ 11. What is the "therefore" there for in 5:1?

👁 12. Who are we to be, and who are we?

👁 13. How are we to walk?

👁 14. What has Christ done?

❤ 15. Going back to question 4, how do verses 4:32-5:2 help you to put away these sins with which you struggle?

❤ 16. What are some things you can do to better enable you to imitate God and walk in love?

Notes

This week, pray each day to be an imitator of God, his beloved child, walking in love.

Pray.

Read Ephesians 4:17-5:21.

Ephesians 5:1-5

✦ 1. Write in your own words how a Christian should live according to verse 1-2.

✦ 2. To what does "Christ loved us and gave himself up for us" refer?

✦ 3. What does it mean that Christ was "a fragrant offering and sacrifice to God"? (See Genesis 8:20-21 and Hebrews 10: 10-18.)

✦ 4. Jesus is held up in verses 1-2 as an example for us, but he is also more than an example. How does Christ Jesus' act of sacrificing himself for sinners like us free us up and enable us to imitate him and walk in love? Remember 2:4-10. (See also Romans 8:1-4.)

👁 5. What does Paul contrast with walking in love?

👁 6. Why must these things not even be named among you?

👁 7. In verse 4, what does Paul prohibit and why?

✦ 8. Why is it not walking in love when we do the things listed in verses 3-4? How are they unloving?

👁 9. What are believers to do instead?

👁 10. Why should one not be sexually immoral, impure, or covetous?

✦ 11. How are filthiness, foolish talk, and crude joking related to sexual immorality, impurity, and covetousness?

✦ 12. How is covetousness idolatry?

✦ 13. Why would Paul contrast thanksgiving with the sins he has listed?

✦ 14. Why would the sexually immoral, the impure, and the covetous have no inheritance in the kingdom of Christ and God? (Are these unforgivable sins?)

♥ 15. Can you identify any sexual immorality, impurity, covetousness, or course talk and joking in your life? With which of these do you struggle? (Remember to examine your thought-life and media input as you consider this question.)

♥ 16. How can thankfulness help you overcome these sins?

Day 2

Pray.

Read Ephesians 5:1-21.

Ephesians 5:6-10

👁 1. What is Paul's warning in verse 6?

👁 2. Why is Paul concerned that believers not be deceived?

✦ 3. What do "these things" refer to?

✦ 4. Why is God's wrath aroused by "these things"?

✦ 5. With whom should we not become partners?

👁 6. Why should we not become partners with these people?

👁 7. How are we to walk, and why?

👁 8. What are we to try to discern?

✦ 9. Why do you think Paul uses the metaphors of darkness and light? What does each of them suggest?

❤ 10. What are some ways we can listen to empty words and be deceived in these areas?

❤ 11. How can you keep from being deceived?

❤ 12. How can you walk as a child of the light and grow in discernment?

♥ 13. What can church bodies do to keep deception out and not become partners with the world?

♥ 14. Why is it important for the church to be a beacon of light, and what does the morality of individual members of the church have to do with this?

♥ 15. What can a church do to keep its light brightly shining?

Day 3

Pray.

Read Ephesians 5:1-21.

Ephesians 5:11-14

👁 1. What are we not only to take no part in but also to expose?

👁 2. What is shameful?

👁 3. What happens to things exposed by the light?

✦ 4. In verse 14, Paul references what is probably a combination of Old Testament passages like Isaiah 60:1.⁵ What happens when light is shone on someone who is sleeping?

👁 5. Who is the light at the end of verse 14?

✦ 6. Why should Christians expose the unfruitful works of darkness? What is Paul suggesting can happen when someone in darkness is exposed to the truth of Jesus? (See also Isaiah 60:1-3 and Luke 1:78-79.)

✦ 7. What does Paul mean when he tells us not to partner with those in the darkness (v 7), to take no part in their unfruitful works (v 11), and not even to speak of what they do (v 12)? Is he telling us to completely separate from the world, or does he mean something else?

 8. What are some ways we can expose darkness in the world?

♥ 9. Based on these verses, how should we treat a brother or sister in our church who is engaging in these sins? What should our goal with him or her be? How and when does church discipline apply to such cases?

♥ 10. What kind of effect can a church full of believers walking as children of the light have on the world around them?

Day 4

Pray.

Read Ephesians 5:1-21.

Ephesians 5:15-17

👁 1. How are believers to walk?

✝ 2. For what is the word "walk" a metaphor?

👁 3. What is the wise way to use time? Why?

👁 4. How does verse 17 further define wisdom?

✦ 5. Considering the verses we have already studied this week, why is it important for believers to live wisely?

✦ 6. The Greek phrase for "making the best use of" can also mean "redeem" or "purchase".[6] How does one make the best use of or redeem time? And how is wisdom related to this?

✦ 7. What do the days being evil have to do with it?

✦ 8. Considering the context, what does it mean to understand what the will of the Lord is? (Does this refer to knowing specifically what God wants for your future, or understanding God's will as it has been revealed in Scripture, or both?) Read Deuteronomy 29:29.

✦ 9. What does understanding the Lord's will have to do with not being foolish but being wise? (See also Colossians 1:9-10.)

♥ 10. How can we come to understand the will of the Lord? (See Romans 12:2.)

♥ 11. What can we know for certain about the will of the Lord? (Read Micah 6:8; Matthew 28:19-20; Romans 8:28; and 1 Thessalonians 4:3.)

♥ 12. What are some of the means God gives us to make decisions about what we think the Lord's will is for us in particular situations?

♥ 13. How are you doing with time? On what do you waste it? How do you make the best use of it?

♥ 14. Considering the verses we read that tell us what the will of the Lord is, what can you do to make the best use of your time?

Day 5

Pray.

Read Ephesians 5:1-21.

Ephesians 5:18-21

👁 1. What does Paul tell the Ephesian Christians not to do, and what does he contrast it with?

👁 2. What are the four things in verses 19-21 that result from being filled with the Spirit?

✦ 3. What do you think addressing one another in psalms, hymns, and spiritual songs means? (Is this when we see one another on the street or does it refer to the gathered assembly of the church?)

✦ 4. What does the heart have to do with "singing and making melody to the Lord"?

✦ 5. Considering verse 19, what aspects are necessary in the corporate singing of a church?

✦ 6. How is the content of what is sung important?

♥ 7. When you sing at the corporate gathering, is your aim "addressing one another"? Do you sing loudly and joyfully enough for others to hear you and be encouraged? Do you sing from the heart?

♥ 8. If you participate in leading the singing at your church, are you facilitating believers "addressing one another"? Ask yourself: is the musical accompaniment drowning out the voices of the congregation? Are the songs difficult to sing? Is there robust congregational singing, or is the congregation just being entertained?

👁 9. How often and for what does Paul tell the Ephesian Christians to give thanks?

10. How can Paul, who is in prison, tell the Ephesian Christians to give thanks always and for everything? How can Paul be thankful for his imprisonment?

 11. How can a believer give thanks even in the midst of difficult circumstances?

12. When do you find it hard to give thanks?

13. Write yourself a note about how to trust God and be thankful for these hard providences.

14. What motivates Christians to submit to one another?

15. What does it mean to submit to one another?

♥ 16. When you are in disagreement with someone else, how do you handle it? Are you happy to follow someone else's lead?

♥ 17. Think about addressing one another in songs, giving thanks, and submitting to one another. How filled are you with the Holy Spirit? How filled is your church?

Notes

This week pray for a submissive attitude toward the Lord and others.

Pray.

Read Ephesians 5.

Ephesians 5:22-24

👁 1. Whom is Paul addressing, and what is he telling them to do?

👁 2. In what way are wives to submit to their husbands?

👁 3. Why are wives called to submit to their husbands?

👁 4. How are wives to submit to their husbands?

✦ 5. What does it mean for a wife to submit to her husband?

✦ 6. Why is the phrase "as to the Lord" in verse 22 important? (See also 1 Peter 3:1-6.)

✦ 7. Some would argue based on 5:21 that husbands and wives are to mutually submit to one another. What evidence do you find in verses 22-24 and the surrounding context that would suggest an authority structure in marriage? (See also 1 Corinthians 11:3.)

✦ 8. Verse 24 says, "wives should submit in everything to their husbands." Do you agree with the following statements? Why or why not?

a. Wives cannot disagree with their husbands.

b. Wives might have to go along with decisions they think are foolish.

c. Wives can or must engage in sin if the husband asks.

d. Wives must submit to verbal or physical abuse.

✦ 9. Is a wife's submission conditional upon a husband loving his wife well? Discuss whether or not submission is only required in a Christian marriage in which the husband loves his wife as Christ loves the church. Read 1 Peter 3:1-2.

✦ 10. What analogy does Paul use for husbands and wives?

✦ 11. Describe what a marriage should look like based on verse 23 and 4:15-16.

♥ 12. If you are married, can you think of a time when you submitted to your husband even though it was difficult?

♥ 13. Can you think of a time you didn't submit "as to the Lord"?

♥ 14. In what areas do you struggle with submitting to your husband?

♥ 15. If you are unmarried and would like to be married, how can you cultivate an attitude of submissiveness that will carry over into your marriage?

♥ 16. How does knowing you will need to submit to the man you marry affect the character traits you desire in a husband?

Day 2

Pray.

Read Ephesians 5:21-6:9.

Ephesians 5:25-33

👁 1. What is Paul's command to husbands?

👁 2. How are husbands to love their wives?

👁 3. What did Christ do for the church, and why did he do it?

✦ 4. Write in your own words a description of how Christ loved the church and what his purpose for the church was in so doing.

✦ 5. Verse 28 begins, "In the same way." Write how a husband's love and purpose for his wife should mirror that of Christ.

👁 6. How should husbands love their wives according to verse 28?

👁 7. How does one treat his own flesh?

✦ 8. In your own words, describe this kind of love.

♥ 9. Reading back over your answers to questions 6 and 8, if you are unmarried and want to be married, what kind of characteristics do you think are important for husbands?

♥ 10. If you are married, write down some of the Christ-like characteristics in your husband for which you are thankful.

♥ 11. If your husband is not very good at self-sacrificial love, go to the Lord and ask him to do a work in your husband's heart. Get help from wise counselors if need be.

✦ 12. What is the "Therefore" in verse 31 referring to?

👁 13. What is the man supposed to do?

👁 14. What do the two become?

✦ 15. What does it mean to become one flesh? Read Genesis 2:18-25.

✦ 16. Paul calls this a mystery, meaning something that was hidden but is now revealed. Look back through verses 22-32 and describe how a marriage mirrors Christ and his church.

✦ 17. Why does Paul call this profound?

👁 18. How does Paul sum up the husband's and wife's duties to one another?

✦ 19. Marriage is a picture of Christ's relationship with his church. What does this suggest about the intimacy and fruitfulness of Christ and the church? What does it suggest about Christ's love and faithfulness?

Day 3

Pray.

Read Ephesians 5:15-6:4.

Ephesians 6:1-4

👁 1. What are children to do?

👁 2. How and why are children to obey their parents?

✦ 3. What does it mean to obey your parents "in the Lord"?

✦ 4. What makes obedience "right"?

👁 5. How is the command restated in verse 2?

✦ 6. How would you compare obeying and honoring?

👁 7. What is the promise that goes with obeying this command?

👁 8. This command is one of the Ten Commandments from Exodus 20:12. What does Paul insert in the middle of the quote?

✦ 9. In the Old Testament, a child who cursed or struck a parent was to be put to death (Exodus 21:15, 17). Paul emphasizes that obeying parents "is right," and that the command comes with a promise. Why is this such an important commandment?

✦ 10. God put the people of Israel in a particular place and promised them blessing. Christians don't live in a particular land today. How does the promise that goes along with this command apply today?

♥ 11. If you are a child dependent on your parents, how are you doing at obeying them? When is it hard? Do you take this command seriously?

♥ 12. If you are an adult, how can you still seek to honor your parents?

◉ 13. How does Paul instruct fathers?

✦ 14. Why do you think Paul specifically addresses fathers instead of both parents? Does this command apply to mothers as well?

♥ 15. If you are a parent, do you recognize ways you provoke your children? What can you do about this?

✦ 16. What does it mean to bring children up in the "discipline and instruction of the Lord"?

♥ 17. If you are a parent, at which of these do you need to work harder? How can you be more consistent in discipline? How can you be more faithful in instruction?

Day 4

Pray.

Read Ephesians 5:15-21; 6:5-9.

Ephesians 6:5-9

👁 1. What is Paul's command to slaves?

👁 2. How are they to obey?

✦ 3. What is the difference between obeying "by the way of eye-service, as people pleasers" and obeying "with a sincere heart," rendering good service "as to the Lord"?

👁 4. What reward is promised for doing good?

✦ 5. How does this reward motivate good service?

✦ 6. Paul does not condone slavery in these verses; rather, he regulates it. In fact, he lists "enslavers" as ungodly sinners in 1 Timothy 1:10. He was speaking into a culture in which slaves made up an estimated one-third of the population.[7] To whom can we apply these verses today?

♥ 7. If you are an employee, do you work "as to the Lord" or "by the way of eye-service"? In what ways do you struggle with your attitude toward work?

♥ 8. How can you greater glorify God at work?

👁 9. What are masters to do?

👁 10. What are masters to know?

✦ 11. What does it mean to "do the same" to slaves?

✦ 12. How does knowing that both slaves and masters serve the same God, and that God considers both slaves and masters as equals, motivate masters to treat slaves well?

♥ 13. If you have someone working under you, is there anything you need to change in your treatment of him or her? What should your goal for that person be?

♥ 14. Consider store clerks, handymen, and others who render you service. How can you treat them in God-honoring ways?

Day 5

Pray.

Read Ephesians 5:1-2, 15-33; 6:1-9.

✦ 1. Paul calls us as Christians to be imitators of God, as his beloved children, walking wisely in love, making the most of the time and being filled with the Holy Spirit. Why do you think he then chooses to address submission in detail?

✦ 2. As you read each of the commands to submission—wives, children, slaves—what parallels do you notice? What conclusions can you draw from these parallels?

✦ 3. As you read the commands to those who are in positions of authority—husbands, fathers, masters—what parallels do you notice? What conclusions can you draw from these parallels?

✦ 4. How is submission imitating God and walking in love "as Christ loved us and gave himself up for us" (5:2)? (See also Philippians 2:3-6.)

✦ 5. What does submission have to do with being filled with the Spirit in verse 18?

♥ 6. Were you convicted by anything in the verses you studied this week? Confess your sins to the Lord, for "he is faithful and just to forgive us our sins and to cleanse us from all unrighteousness" (1 John 1:9). Jesus died for head-strong wives, disobedient children, sinful mothers, dishonest slaves, and cruel masters. And he sent the Holy Spirit to fill us, enabling us to obey.

Notes

This week pray each day that you would stand firm, resisting the schemes of the devil, and pray for all the saints to boldly proclaim the mystery of the gospel.

Pray.

Read Ephesians 1 and 6:10-24.

Ephesians 6:10-13

1. In conclusion, what does Paul exhort the Ephesian Christians to do?

2. Considering the culture and circumstances into which this letter was written and considering what is written in this letter, why do the Ephesian Christians need to be strong?

3. Paul instructs the Ephesian Christians to be strong, but they are to be strong "in the Lord and in the strength of his might." Who, then, is doing the work of being strong?

4. What are the Ephesian Christians to put on?

5. Why are they to put on this armor?

6. Who is the devil, and what will be his end? Read Genesis 3:13-15; Ephesians 2:2; Colossians 2:13-15; 1 Peter 5:8; and Revelation 20:10.

7. Against whom do Christians wrestle?

8. What are these spiritual forces of evil trying to do? Read Job 1:6-12; Matthew 4:8-11; Mark 4:14-15; and Revelation 12:9-12; 13:5-8.

9. Whom do we not wrestle against?

10. Why is it important to know we don't wrestle against flesh and blood?

11. Why ultimately should the Christian take up the whole armor of God?

12. To what does the evil day refer? Read Ephesians 2:2 and 5:16.

13. What does standing firm against the devil have to do with the "deceitful schemes" and "speaking the truth in love" discussed in 4:14-15?

14. How does knowing that you don't wrestle against flesh and blood help you love your enemies?

15. Having read this letter from the beginning, what do you think Paul means when he writes, "having done all, to stand firm"? In other words, what "all" do the Ephesian Christians need to do, and what does it mean for them to "stand firm"?

✦ 16. Paul exhorts the Ephesian Christians to be strong in verse 10 just as he prayed for them to be strengthened in 3:16. How does Paul's prayer in 3:14-21 shed light on how to "be strong in the Lord"?

♥ 17. What means are you using (or do you need to use) to be strong in the Lord?

♥ 18. Discuss how you can tend to rely on your own strength rather than being strong "in the strength of his might."

Day 2

Pray.

Read Ephesians 6:10-24.

Ephesians 6:14-17

👁 1. Paul repeats his exhortation for Christians to stand and then describes the armor of God. List the pieces of armor Christians are to put on.

✦ 2. The belt of a Roman soldier not only held his garments secure, but also had a metal apron that hung down to protect the soldier's lower abdomen and groin. For what is the belt of truth a metaphor? (See John 14:6-7; Ephesians 1:16-21; 2 Timothy 2:12-14; and 1 Peter 1:13.)

♥ 3. How committed are you to growing in your knowledge of God? What means are you using? How are you girding yourself against false doctrine?

✦ 4. The soldier's breastplate would protect his heart and other vital organs. What does the "breastplate of righteousness" symbolize? (See Isaiah 59:16-17; 61:10-11; Romans 6:12-14; Philippians 3:9; and Revelation 19:8.)

♥ 5. How are you protecting your heart? Do you rest in the righteousness of Christ? At the same time, are you regularly repenting of and fighting against sin? Do you have other women who keep you accountable?

✦ 6. Shoes protect a soldier's feet, keep him from slipping, and enable him to quickly reach his destination. What spiritual truths do the shoes in verse 15 stand for? (See Isaiah 52:6-7; Romans 10:14-17; and 2 Corinthians 5:18-21.)

♥ 7. How well do you know the gospel? Are you ready and looking for opportunities to share it?

✦ 8. Shields would be soaked in water so they could extinguish flaming arrows. How does the "shield of faith" extinguish "the flaming darts of the evil one"? (See Genesis 15:1; 2 Samuel 22:31; Psalm 3:3-4; 28:7; Hebrews 11:24-26; 12:1-2; and 1 John 5:4-5.)

✦ 9. What do the "flaming darts of the evil one" refer to? (See the verses from Day 1, Question 8.)

♥ 10. What are some flaming darts in your life? How can you fight back with faith?

✦ 11. A soldier's helmet protects his head. What does the "helmet of salvation" do? (See Isaiah 59:16-20; John 10:27-29; 1 Thessalonians 5:8-11; and 1 Peter 1:13.)

♥ 12. How does the knowledge of your salvation and the hope you have in Christ help you to stand firm?

👁 13. The "sword of the Spirit" is the only offensive weapon mentioned. What is the sword of the Spirit?

✦ 14. How does the word of God act as the sword of the Spirit? (See Luke 4:1-13; Romans 8:5-14; and Hebrews 4:12-13.)

Grace

♥ 15. Write down a specific time when you were able to use Scripture to fight your sin or discouragement?

♥ 16. How does consistent time in the Scriptures and consistent sitting under the preaching of God's Word help you fight the schemes of the devil?

♥ 17. What can you do to hone your skills at wielding the sword of the Spirit?

Day 3

Pray.

Read Ephesians 6:10-24.

Ephesians 6:18-20

👁 1. When and how does Paul tell Christians to pray?

✟ 2. What does it mean to pray "at all times"? (See Luke 18:1; Colossians 4:2; and 1 Thessalonians 5:16-18.)

✦ 3. What does it mean to pray "in the Spirit"? Read Romans 8:5, 25-27 and Jude 20-21.

✦ 4. What is "prayer and supplication"?

✦ 5. To what "end" does Paul say to "keep alert with all perseverance"?

✦ 6. Why would Paul tell Christians to "keep alert with all perseverance"? (See also Mark 13:32-37.)

👁 7. For whom are Christians to make supplication?

✦ 8. Whom does Paul mean by "all the saints"?

👁 9. What does Paul ask prayer for?

✛ 10. Paul does not ask the Ephesian Christians to pray for his release from prison. What can you conclude about Paul from his prayer request? What is most important to him?

✛ 11. What does prayer for ourselves and other saints have to do with the armor of God?

♥ 12. How often do you pray? Based on this, are you staying alert?

♥ 13. What are your priorities in prayer? Are you praying in the Spirit? Would someone listening to your prayers think you are wrestling against the "spiritual forces of evil" or against "flesh and blood"?

♥ 14. How can you make supplication for all the saints?

♥ 15. Do you pray regularly for particular pastors and missionaries to boldly proclaim the gospel?

Day 4

Pray.

Read Ephesians 6:10-24.

✚ 1. Who provides the armor of God?

✚ 2. Who wears and wields the armor of God?

✚ 3. What does this tell you about God's work and our responsibilities in the war against evil?

♥ 4. The Christian needs all of the armor of God along with much prayer to be strong in the Lord and stand firm. After considering the pieces of armor, where are you most vulnerable to attack? What can you do about this vulnerability?

Ephesians 6:21-24

👁 5. Why has Paul sent Tychicus?

👁 6. How is Tychicus described? (See also Acts 20:4: Colossians 4:7; 2 Timothy 4:12; and Titus 3:12.)

✦ 7. What do verses 21-22 tell you about Paul's relationship with the Ephesian Christians?

♥ 8. How are your relationships within your church? Do you have beloved brothers and sisters who are involved in your life? How can you cultivate more intimate relationships with others in your church?

♥ 9. Do you desire and strive to encourage the hearts of other believers? Whom do you seek to encourage in your church? How do you encourage them?

◉ 10. Paul began his letter with grace and peace. How does he end his letter?

✝ 11. How are Paul's wishes for peace and grace for the Ephesian Christians appropriate for the conclusion of this letter?

✝ 12. How is Paul's repeated mention of love in these last verses also fitting for the conclusion of this letter?

✝ 13. What does it mean to "love our Lord Jesus Christ with love incorruptible"? From where does the love actually come (v 23)? (See also Jude 1-2.)

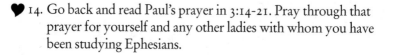14. Go back and read Paul's prayer in 3:14-21. Pray through that prayer for yourself and any other ladies with whom you have been studying Ephesians.

Day 5

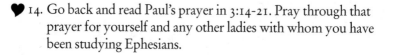1. Prayerfully read back through Ephesians and skim through the various weeks' studies. What lessons stand out for you? How are you going to put into practice what you have learned in your study of Ephesians?

Notes

Notes

FAITH: A Bible Study on James for Women

bit.ly/FaithStudy

JOY! – A Bible Study on Philippians for Women

bit.ly/JoyStudy

Inductive Bible studies for women by Keri Folmar
endorsed by...

Kathleen Nielson is author of the *Living Word Bible Studies*; Director of Women's Initiatives, The Gospel Coalition; and wife of Niel, who served as President of Covenant College from 2002 to 2012.

Diane Schreiner is the mother of four grown children and has led women's Bible studies for more than 20 years. She is the wife of Tom Schreiner, an author and pastor who serves at Southern Baptist Theological Seminary as Professor of New Testament Interpretation, Professor of Biblical Theology, and Associate Dean of the School of Theology.

Connie Dever is author of *The Praise Factory* children's ministry curriculum and wife of Pastor Mark Dever, President of 9 Marks Ministries

Kristie Anyabwile, holds a history degree from NC State University, and is married to Thabiti, Assistant Pastor for Church Planting at Capitol Hill Baptist Church in Washington DC, and a Council Member for The Gospel Coalition.

Gloria Furman is a pastor's wife in the Middle East and author of *Glimpses of Grace* and *Treasuring Christ When Your Hands Are Full.*

"It is hard to imagine a better inductive Bible study tool than this one."
–Diane Schreiner

Knowable Word
Helping Ordinary People Learn to Study the Bible

by Peter Krol
Foreword by Tedd Tripp

Observe...Interpret...Apply

Simple concepts at the heart of good Bible study. Learn the basics in a few minutes—gain skills for a lifetime. The spiritual payoff is huge.

Ready?

117 pages — *Learn more at bit.ly/Knowable*

"Peter Krol has done us a great service by writing the book *Knowable Word*. It is valuable for those who have never done in-depth Bible study and a good review for those who have. I look forward to using this book to improve my own Bible study.'"
Jerry Bridges, author, **The Pursuit of Holiness,** *and many more*

"It is hard to over-estimate the value of this tidy volume. It is clear and uncomplicated. No one will be off-put by this book. It will engage the novice and the serious student of Scripture. It works as a solid read for individuals or as an exciting study for a small group."
Tedd Tripp, pastor and author (from the Foreword)

"At the heart of *Knowable Word* is a glorious and crucial conviction: that understanding the Bible is not the preserve of a few, but the privilege and joy of all God's people. Peter Krol's book demystifies the process of reading God's Word and in so doing enfranchises the people of God. I warmly encourage you to read it. Better still, read it with others and apply its method together."
Dr. Tim Chester, The Porterbrook Network

"Here is an excellent practical guide to interpreting the Bible. Krol has thought through, tested, and illustrated in a clear, accessible way basic steps in interpreting the Bible, and made everything available in a way that will encourage ordinary people to deepen their own study."
Vern Poythress, Westminster Theological Seminary

"This book has three primary virtues and many secondary ones. Its primary virtues are the nobility of its goal..., the accuracy of the proposed methodology for interacting with the Bible, and the practical approach to the subject. Additionally, this book does a splendid job of employing the practice of 'learning by doing.'"
Leland Ryken, author, **How to Read the Bible as Literature**

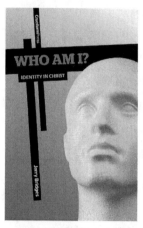

Who Am I?
Identity in Christ

by Jerry Bridges

Jerry Bridges unpacks Scripture to give the Christian eight clear, simple, interlocking answers to one of the most essential questions of life.

Also available as an audiobook read by Alistair Begg

Learn more at bit.ly/WHOAMI

"Jerry Bridges' gift for simple but deep spiritual communication is fully displayed in this warm-hearted, biblical spelling out of the Christian's true identity in Christ."

J. I. Packer, *Theological Editor*, ESV Study Bible; *author*, Knowing God, A Quest for Godliness, Concise Theology

"I know of no one better prepared than Jerry Bridges to write *Who Am I?* He is a man who knows who he is in Christ and he helps us to see succinctly and clearly who we are to be. Thank you for another gift to the Church of your wisdom and insight in this book."

R.C. Sproul, *founder, chairman, president, Ligonier Ministries; executive editor*, Tabletalk *magazine; general editor*, The Reformation Study Bible

"*Who Am I?* answers one of the most pressing questions of our time in clear gospel categories straight from the Bible. This little book is a great resource to ground new believers and remind all of us of what God has made us through faith in Jesus. Thank the Lord for Jerry Bridges, who continues to provide the warm, clear, and biblically balanced teaching that has made him so beloved to this generation of Christians."

Richard D. Phillips, *Senior Minister, Second Presbyterian Church, Greenville, SC*

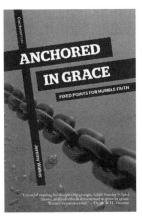

Anchored in Grace
Fixed Points for Humble Faith

by Jeremy Walker

Clear truths from Scripture...

**Central. Humbling. Saving.
Comforting. God-glorifying.**

Get Anchored.

86 pages
bit.ly/ANCHRD

"Rarely does the title of a book so clearly represent its contents as does this one. With brevity and precision, Jeremy Walker sets forth God's work of salvation in the believer from beginning to end. In a day when there is so much confusion regarding even the most fundamental truths of redemption, this concise yet comprehensive work is a clear beacon of light to guide the seeker and to instruct and comfort the believer."
Paul David Washer, Director, HeartCry Missionary Society

"As a pastor, I am always looking for a book that is brief, simple, and biblical in its presentation of the God-exalting doctrines of grace to put into the hands of believers. I think my search is now over! Jeremy Walker provides us with a book that shows us in small compass how God's grace has turned wretched sinners into heaven-bound saints. Wonderful!"
Conrad Mbewe, pastor, Kabwata Baptist Church; Chancellor, African Christian University, Lusaka, Zambia

"Crisp, clear, concise, and biblical, Walker's book offers up the doctrines of God's grace in a manner persuasive to the mind and powerful to the heart."
Dr. Joel R. Beeke, President, Puritan Reformed Theological Seminary

"A sure-footed journey...a trusted guide. Reading this book will both thrill and convict, challenge and confirm. Essential reading for discipleship groups, Adult Sunday School classes, and individuals determined to grow in grace. Warmly recommended."
Derek W. H. Thomas, Professor, Reformed Theological Seminary

""This is a meaty feast of solid doctrinal truth crammed into a short, pointed, and applied book. The deeply encouraging doctrines of grace are opened up to us and explained clearly. This is historical, biblical truth brought back into the light for the modern Christian. Everyone's a winner with this one."
Mez McConnell, author; Senior Pastor of Niddrie Community Church, Edinburgh, Scotland; and founder and ministry director of 20schemes

Friends and Lovers
Cultivating Companionship and Intimacy in Marriage
by Joel R. Beeke

Marriage is for God's glory and our good.

The secret? Intimate Christian companionship.

96 pages – Learn more at bit.ly/FriendsAnd

"A book about love, marriage, and sex from Joel Beeke that is surprisingly candid yet without a trace of smuttiness. Fresh and refreshingly straightforward, this is the best book of its kind."
Derek W H Thomas, Visiting Professor, Reformed Theological Seminary

"Marriage is hard work. And wonderful. And sometimes, it's both at the same time. *Friends and Lovers* is like a personal mentoring session on marriage with a man whose heart is devoted to seeing Christ honored in how we love each other as husbands and wives. It's full of practical wisdom and grace. A delight."
Bob Lepine, Co-Host, FamilyLife Today

"By laying the theological, emotional, social, and spiritual foundations of marriage before heading to the bedroom, Joel Beeke provides a healthy corrective to the excessive and obsessive sex-focus of our generation and even of some pastors. But, thankfully, he also goes on to provide wise, practical, down-to-earth direction for couples wanting to discover or recover physical intimacy that will both satisfy themselves and honor God."
Dr. David Murray, Professor, Puritan Reformed Theological Seminary

"There is no better book than this to renew the affection of happy marriage."
Geoffrey Thomas, Pastor, Alfred Place Baptist Church, Wales

"The pure delight our ancient parents had in each other, touching every aspect of their lives together, was sadly lost at the fall. What this book powerfully shows through the teaching of the Scriptures, though, is that this delight is recoverable to a great degree in Christ. I appreciated enormously the way in which the divine gift of human sexuality is handled, with biblical honesty but without any pandering to our culture's prurient ways."
Michael A.G. Haykin, Professor of Church History and Biblical Spirituality, The Southern Baptist Theological Seminary

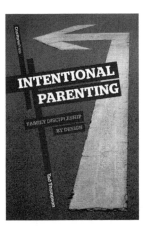

Intentional Parenting
Family Discipleship by Design
by Tad Thompson

The Big Picture and a Simple Plan — That's What You Need to Do Family Discipleship Well

This book will allow you to take all the sermons, teachings, and exhortations you have received on the topic of family discipleship, make sense of it, and put it to use.

Learn more at bit.ly/IParent

"As parents, we know God has given us the responsibility to train our children in his ways. But many parents don't know where or how to start. Tad has done us all a favor by identifying seven key categories of biblical teaching we can utilize in teaching our children godly truth and principles. This easy-to-follow plan will help any parent put the truth of God's Word into their children's hearts."
Kevin Ezell, President, North American Mission Board, Southern Baptist Convention; father of six

"Dr. Tad Thompson's *Intentional Parenting* is a practical page-turner that encourages fathers to engage the hearts of their families with truth and grace. In an age when truth is either ignored or despised, it is refreshing to see a book written for ordinary fathers who want their families to be sanctified by the truth. Thompson writes with a grace which reminds us that parenting flows from the sweet mercies of Christ."
Joel Beeke, President, Puritan Reformed Theological Seminary

"Need an introductory text to the topic of discipling children? Here is a clear, simple book on family discipleship, centered on the gospel rather than human successes or external behaviors."
Timothy Paul Jones, Ph.D., Professor of Discipleship and Family Ministry at The Southern Baptist Theological Seminary and author of Family Ministry Field Guide, Perspectives on Family Ministry, and Trained in the Fear of God: Family Ministry in Biblical, Theological, and Practical Perspective

"Tad Thompson knows about the needs of today's families. This approach is creative, thoroughly biblical, and is a must read for any parent who desires for the children to love God with all their heart, with all their soul, and with all their might. This is a great strategy for anyone who is looking for a way to pull their family together around God's Word."
Blake Gideon, Senior Pastor, First Baptist Church, Inola, Oklahoma

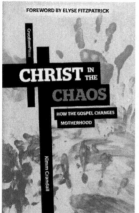

Christ in the Chaos
How the Gospel Changes Motherhood

by Kimm Crandall

FOREWORD BY ELYSE FITZPATRICK

MOMS:
- **Stop comparing yourself to others.**
- **Stop striving to meet false expectations.**
- **Stop thinking your performance dictates your worth.**
- **Instead, look to the gospel for rest, joy, sufficiency, identity, and motivation.**

Learn more at bit.ly/Christ-in

"Although Kimm Crandall's message would revive any soul longing for the breath of the gospel of grace, I am especially eager to recommend this book to that heart who strives to know God and to make him known to the little ones who call her 'Momma.' Kimm is a candid and gracious fellow sojourner, faithfully pointing to God's immeasurable steadfast love and grace in the midst of our mess."

**Lauren Chandler, wife of Matt Chandler (pastor of The Village Church),
mother of three, writer, singer, and speaker**

"What an amazingly wild and wise, disruptive and delighting, freeing and focusing book. Kimm's book is for every parent willing to take the stewardship of children and the riches of the gospel seriously. This is one of the most helpful and encouraging books on parenting I've read in the past twenty years. Kimm writes as a multi-child mom and a grace-saturated woman who understands the exhausting demands of good parenting and the inexhaustible supply of God's grace. This will be a book you will want to give to parents, to-be parents, and grandparents."

Scotty Smith, author; Founding Pastor, Christ Community Church

"Jesus' yoke is easy and his burden is light. Why, then, as a mom did I feel as if I were carrying the weight of the world and these children on my shoulders alone? I had forgotten the gospel and instead was piling on the 'have-to's' that promised to fulfill me as a wife, give me purpose as a mother, and produce guaranteed spiritual kids. I just wish I had read and absorbed the truths that Kimm so gently reminds us of."

Kendra Fletcher, Homeschool mom of 8; blogger, PreschoolersAndPeace.com

"Kimm gives us the truth of free grace that unshackles us from trying to be Mom of the Year, and shows us how the gospel changes motherhood from drudgery to joy. I pray each mom who finds this book becomes more aware of how Christ's love for her changes everything about her."

Jessica Thompson, coauthor of Give them Grace

Inheritance of Tears
Trusting the Lord of Life When Death Visits the Womb

by Jessalyn Hutto

Miscarriage: Deeply traumatic, tragically common...and so often misunderstood or trivialized.

The gospel can make all the difference to suffering mothers.

Learn more at bit.ly/OFTEARS

"We wish there had been good Christian books on miscarriage available when we faced that terrible trial. This book is written out of deep suffering, but with an even deeper sense of hope. This book can help you think and pray if you have faced miscarriage, and it can help you understand how to minister to someone who has grieving women in your local church."
Russel and Maria Moore, Russel Moore is President of the Ethics and Religious Liberty Commission of the Southern Baptist Convention

"This book is equally important for those who have suffered miscarriage and those who have not. Rarely is the topic of miscarriage addressed with such candor and depth. Deeply personal and brave.... May her words minister to many."
Jen Wilkin, author, *Women of the Word* (Crossway)

"Comforting, biblical, helpful...a needed word for anyone who has experienced this great loss. A great resource for the church."
Trillia Newbell, author of *Fear and Faith* (2015) and *United* (2014)

"Many women grasp for hope in the overwhelming days of grief that follow miscarriage. I have twice been that woman, and Jessalyn Hutto has written the book I wish I'd had as I walked through the pain. This book will be a healing balm to grieving women."
Courtney Reissig, wife; mom; author, The Accidental Feminist

"Miscarriage? Don't talk about it. Sadly, this is the approach many churches take. As a result, the woman in the pew suffers unbearable pain and grieves all alone. Change must happen, and *Inheritance of Tears* is the place to start.."
Matthew Barrett, Executive Editor, Credo Magazine

"She guides us theologically, so that we see God's wisdom, God's purpose, and God's love in the midst of our suffering. I gladly recommend this work to others."
Tom Schreiner, The Southern Baptist Theological Seminary

The Company We Keep
In Search of Biblical Friendship

by Jonathan Holmes
Foreword by Ed Welch

Biblical friendship is deep, honest, pure, tranparent, and liberating.

It is also attainable.

112 pages
bit.ly/B-Friend

"Jonathan Holmes has the enviable ability to say a great deal in a few words. Here is a wonderful primer on the nature of biblical friendship—what it means and why it matters."
Alistair Begg, Truth for Life; Senior Pastor, Parkside Church

"Jonathan has succeeded in giving us a picture of how normal, daily, biblical friendships can be used by God to mold us into the likeness of Christ. If you want a solid, fresh way of re-thinking all of your relationships, read this book."
Dr. Tim S. Lane, co-author, How People Change

"Jonathan has made a significant contribution to the Kingdom. We expect far too little from our friendships, and Jonathan's work not only encourages us to expect more, it also equips us to give more. His four marks of biblical friendship—constancy, candor, carefulness, and counsel—provide a robust and relevant GPS for intentional and vulnerable gospel-centered friendships. The 'Dig Deeper' sections embedded in each chapter make this a great book not only for individuals, but also for small groups."
Robert W. Kellemen, Executive Director, Biblical Counseling Coalition

"Short. Thoughtful. Biblical. Practical. I'm planning to get my friends to read this book so we can transform our friendships into something more biblical. I am grateful to Jonathan for carefully helping us think through the topic of Christian friendships."
Deepak Reju, Pastor of Biblical Counseling, Capitol Hill Baptist Church, Washington, DC

"I talk with many Christians who have intensely practical questions about how to make and maintain friendships with their fellow believers. Jonathan Holmes' book is filled with answers that are equally down-to-earth, nitty-gritty, and specific. This is a book that isn't just a roadmap for cultivating Christian friendship. It's also a tour guide, taking us where we need to go with warmth and wisdom."
Wesley Hill, author, Washed and Waiting